THE
New York Giants Trivia Book

THE
New York Giants Trivia Book

Michael Lichtenstein

ST. MARTIN'S GRIFFIN
NEW YORK

Design by Basha Zapatka

ISBN 0-312-13131-3

First St. Martin's Griffin Edition: August 1995
10 9 8 7 6 5 4 3 2 1

For my parents, Molly and Irving,
who were always there,
and to all those Giants fans
who waited 18 years,
1963–1981

ACKNOWLEDGMENTS

For all those who supported me with their friendship, kindness, and often with their wisdom: my "brother," Steve Shestakofsky; my buddies Mel Watkins, Michael Anderson, Rich Nicholls, David Kelly, Jim English, Tony Mendillo, and Arline Youngman; Kris Ensminger and those great cookies, Susan Fromberg Schaeffer, Judith Spindler, Judy Miceli, and Phyllis Gelfand; my former boss at the *New York Times Book Review*, Rebecca Sinkler; the New York Giants for their cooperation in the making of this book; thanks to Dan Rubin, Jerry Pinkus, Aaron Salkind, the New York Giants, the University of Oklahoma, and Georgetown University for the use of their photographs; my St. Martin's Press family of Diane Higgins, Joe Rinaldi, Becky Koh, Andrew Graybill, and Bob Weil; and Janet Shields for just being who she is.

CONTENTS

INTRODUCTION

Reading this book is like perusing a family album. So many wonderful memories! So many true and lasting football heroes!

As a schoolboy in Brooklyn, I had seen the Giants play against the Brooklyn Dodgers at Ebbets Field. (Yes, Brooklyn had a fine NFL team in the 1930s.) I watched Benny Friedman, Mel Hein, Jim Lee Howell, Harry Newman, Ken Strong, and so many of the great old-timers of two-way football. Did you know that I played for the Giants? Well, it was the Jersey City Giants, the farm team for the New York Giants coached by Bill Owen, Steve Owen's brother. I wasn't good enough for the big club, but we did use the Giants A formation and we trained with the New York club. Playing both ways, I was the tailback and signal caller on offense and the safety man in the 6-2-2-1 defense. Merely mentioning those football phrases sends my memory racing back.

That's what this book is all about . . . the good old days. Of course the modern stars like Phil Simms and Lawrence Taylor are in it, too, but for me, those marvelous moments and great players of long ago are especially captivating.

Emlen Tunnell, running back punts at the Polo Grounds; Arnie Weinmeister, number 73, the only number visible in a sea of mud as he had not been on his back all game; Al Blozis, killed in action in World War II only months after wearing a Giants uniform; the day Y. A. Tittle threw seven touchdown passes at Yankee Stadium to tie Sid Luckman's 1943 NFL record; Ken Strong, kicking field goals and points-after; "That's all, brother"; Frank Gifford making all-pro his rookie year as a defensive back while playing offense and defense; the willowy grace of Del Shofner; "the best football game ever played"; the rise to football glory of Phil Simms; Lawrence Taylor's greatest game; Al DeRogatis readjusting his displaced kneecap as he sat on the turf between plays—again and again; and Mel Hein, Eddie Price, Joe Morrison, Kyle Rote, John Cannady, "Tuffy" Leemans, Ward Cuff, Ed

Danowski, Bull Karcis, "Feets" Barnum, Hank Soar, Tom Landry . . . we were in awe of all of them.

The feeling I remember best of all was the joy they took in playing and being together and in projecting that fun and excitement to us.

That's what this book by Michael Lichtenstein is all about—the nostalgia of joy experienced by any football fan, particularly the Giants fan. I commend it to you.

Marty Glickman
April 1995

1

THE EARLY YEARS: 1925–55

Questions:

1. What year was the Giants' inaugural season?

2. The Giants lost the first game in their existence, 14–0. Who was the opponent? a. The Chicago Bears b. The Green Bay Packers c. The Washington Redskins d. The Providence Steam Roller

3. What was the price Tim Mara paid for his NFL franchise, later to be called the Giants?

4. What was Tim Mara's profession?

5. Who was the Giants' first head coach? He had been a college coach for a number of years, most notably at Navy.

6. Who was the Giants' marquee player in their maiden season?

7. In the kickoff season, more than 70,000 fans filled the Polo Grounds for the final game that year. The Giants had been running in the red going into that game, but the huge ticket sales turned the franchise around, and the Giants ended the season in the black. They played the Chicago Bears, who that day featured what legendary all-American halfback from Illinois?

8. When did the Giants appear in their first NFL championship game? a. 1929 b. 1933 c. 1937 d. 1939

9. What game was known as the Sneakers Game?

10. From 1933 through 1945, the Giants appeared in how many championship games? a. 7 b. 3 c. 4 d. 9

11. Who was the Hall of Fame center who anchored the Giants line from 1931 to 1945?

12. Who was the Giants tackle of the late 1920s enshrined in both the NFL Hall of Fame and the Baseball Hall of Fame?

13. During their first twenty seasons, how many league championships did the Giants win? a. 6 b. 1 c. 3 d. 2

14. Who was the standout Giants tackle killed in action during World War II?

15. Which member of the 1941 Giants was presented the Congressional Medal of Honor for heroism in World War II? a. Hank Soar b. Ward Cuff c. Jack Lummus d. Frank Reagan

16. Who played end for the Giants in the 1930s and 1940s and would later be the Giants head coach in the 1950s? a. Will Walls b. Jim Lee Howell c. Vince Dennery d. Ray Poole

17. Who was the native New Yorker who was given a "day" by the Giants at the Polo Grounds in 1943 and then went on to throw seven touchdown passes against the Giants that day? a. Allie Sherman b. Tony Bova c. Sid Luckman d. George Cafego

18. Who coached the Giants from 1931 to 1953?

19. Who was the Giants top rusher of the late 1930s from Oregon? a. Kink Richards b. Red Wolfe c. Alphonse "Tuffy" Leemans d. Bull Karcis

20. Who was the all-around back who led the Giants in scoring from 1937 to 1942? a. Dale Burnett b. Ward Cuff c. Andy Marefos d. Jim Neill

21. Who was the first player selected by the Giants in the initial NFL draft?

22. Who was the Hall of Famer from New York University best known for his kicking in the 1930s and 1940s?

23. Which team were the Giants playing against on December 7, 1941, at the Polo Grounds? a. The Brooklyn Dodgers b. The Philadelphia Eagles c. The Detroit Lions d. The Cleveland Rams

24. Who is the winningest coach in Giants history? a. Allie Sherman b. Bill Parcells c. Steve Owen d. Tim Mara

25. Who was the first African American to play for the Giants?

26. Name the two Giants players from the 1946 team who were suspended from league play for associating with gamblers and failing to report a bribe prior to the NFL title game.

27. True or False: Steve Owen is credited with designing the Umbrella Defense.

28. Name the rookie quarterback acquired from the Redskins in 1948.

29. Who was the Giants assistant coach from the 1950s who would later be the winning head coach in the first two Super Bowls?

30. Match the player with his alma mater:

Charlie Conerly	Texas
Eddie Price	Penn State
Tom Landry	Duke
Roosevelt Grier	Mississippi
Al DeRogatis	Tulane

31. Who was the Columbia University end who led the Giants in receiving from 1948 to 1950? a. Bob McChesney b. Bill Swiacki c. Ellery Williams d. Kelley Mote

32. What year did the Giants select Frank Gifford in the NFL draft?

33. Who holds the record for the longest run from scrimmage by a New York Giant?

34. Which Giants running back ran for 218 yards against the Chicago Cardinals in a game during the 1950 season? a. Gene "Choo-Choo" Roberts b. Kyle Rote c. Frank Gifford d. Eddie Price

35. Who was known as Automatic Ben?

36. Which team was defensive star Andy Robustelli acquired from? a. The Los Angeles Rams b. The Chicago Cardinals c. The Pittsburgh Steelers d. The Brooklyn Dodgers

37. Which Giants defender led the NFL in interceptions in 1951 with 11?

38. Name the Giants kicker who had only one toe on his kicking foot.

39. Name the four-time All-Pro Giants defensive lineman from the early 1950s.

40. Which Giants defensive player served as a player-coach during the 1954 and 1955 seasons? a. Dick Nolan b. Tom Landry c. Pete Mangum d. Emlen Tunnell

41. Who replaced Steve Owen as Giants head coach in 1954?

42. Name the running back who joined the Giants in 1955 from the Canadian Football League.

43. Which Giants defensive lineman from the 1950s and 1960s went on to become an actor, singer, and minister?

44. Who was the unheralded late-round draft choice from Morgan State University who moved in as a starting offensive tackle in 1953 and would end up in the Hall of Fame?

45. Who was the all-American halfback from Southern Methodist University that the Giants converted to wide receiver? a. Forrest Griffith b. Bob Jackson c. Clarence Avinger d. Kyle Rote

"An Empty Store with Chairs in It"

The Legacy lives on: Wellington Mara, son of Giants founder Tim Mara. (Jerry Pinkus)

The year was 1925, the height of the roaring twenties, and Tim Mara was definitely a man about town. He was a successful businessman and bookie (bookmaking was legal during this time) who could count among his friends, if not customers, New York governor Al Smith and New York City mayor Jimmy Walker. Another friend, Billy Gibson, was the manager of heavyweight boxing champion Gene Tunney. Tim Mara wanted to invest in the pugilistic legend, but his contact with Gibson would take his business ventures into uncharted waters. Gibson was conferring with two gentlemen, one being NFL commissioner Joe Carr, about putting New

York on the NFL map. Carr wanted Gibson to put up the money for this new franchise, but Gibson was wary of this venture. Instead, he suggested his friend, Tim Mara, as a possible owner. Mara had never seen a football game in his life, but like any businessman, he asked the price. It was right, and a deal was made. The New York Giants were born.

To this day the actual price of purchasing the franchise is still in question. The figure has ranged from $500 to as much as $2,500, but according to Tim Mara's son, Wellington, when told the price, his father responded, "An empty store with chairs in it is worth that much in New York City."

Despite the warnings from his friend Al Smith that pro football would never make it, Tim Mara hung on to the Giants. That first season Smith's gloomy forecast seemed prophetic until the final home game of the season. The Giants had been running in the red, but the Chicago Bears came to town with the man who could put fans in the stands: Red Grange. More than 70,000 attended that game alone, which was enough to help the Giants finish in the black. Pro football had a toehold in New York.

Tim Mara died in 1959. He lived long enough to see his venture turn into one of the showcase franchises in all professional sports. In 1963 he was inducted into the National Football League Hall of Fame—as a charter member.

A Real Giant Hero

Al Blozis. (Georgetown University)

The winds of war were sweeping the world when Al Blozis graduated from Georgetown University in June 1942.
The Philippines had fallen. The Pacific fleet was still in
shambles at Pearl Harbor. German tanks smashed their

Al Blozis, collegiate record holder in the shot put: the Olympic dream unfulfilled. (Georgetown University)

way through Russia, heading to Stalingrad. And America was mobilizing for the monumental task ahead: the defeat of Japan and Nazi Germany.

Al Blozis had hoped to win a gold medal in the 1940 Summer Olympics in the shot put. Blozis, who stood six-foot-six and weighed 250 pounds, had shattered every shot put record that ever existed for a collegian. But thanks to Hitler and Tojo there would be no Olympic Games in 1940. Al Blozis's disappointment was tempered by the fact that he also played football. He was a tackle in an era when a player played both ways, offense and defense, each game. Blozis joined the Giants for the 1942 season after trying to get into every branch of the military. His great patriotism came up against his only obstacle—his size. Al Blozis was rejected simply because he was too big.

Blozis played the game with the ferocity and drive that marked him as an All-League selection in just his first season. Although he was enjoying tremendous success in football, his quest to join the military never wavered, and finally he was inducted into the army at the end of the 1943 season.

During basic training Al Blozis set a record for throwing a hand grenade. Because of his size Blozis's uniforms had to be specially tailored. He completed Officers Training School in the fall of 1944. The war was getting that much closer for Al Blozis.

Giants coach Steve Owen couldn't believe his good fortune when Lieutenant Al Blozis showed up at the Polo Grounds during his leave after being commissioned. Blozis put on a practice uniform and would play in the next two games, against Brooklyn (Brooklyn had a football team then, called the Dodgers) and the Washington Redskins.

Lieutenant Al Blozis played in the 1944 championship for the Giants against the Green Bay Packers, a game the Giants would lose, 14–7. Shortly thereafter, Al Blozis shipped overseas.

Six weeks after Blozis played in that championship game against Green Bay he went out in a snowstorm in the Vosges Mountains in France to search for a missing patrol and never returned. Al Blozis was listed as missing in action. A number of weeks later the army officially listed him as killed in action. Al Blozis was 26 years old. The Giants retired his jersey. No Giants player will ever wear number 32 again.

The Iron Man of Pro Football

Mel Hein. (New York Giants)

In an era before stadiums, end zone celebrations, salary caps, and league television contracts that could support several small-size nations, pro football players toiled on both sides of the ball. Perhaps no player was more proficient than Mel Hein, a charter member of the NFL Hall of Fame and the center and linebacker for the Giants from 1931 to 1945.

Hein stood six-foot-three and weighed 230 pounds. When he graduated from Washington State University the NFL draft was still several years away, so Hein wrote

to the Giants asking for a tryout. The Giants wisely of-
fered the Washington State All-American a contract, and
the Iron Man's career began.

Mel Hein made All-League eight times and played in
seven championship games. On offense he was a pulver-
izing blocker. As a linebacker, Hein was a deadly tackler
and an alert pass defender. While playing for Washington State he once intercepted eight passes—in a single
game. After Hein hung up the cleats, he coached in the
old All-American Football Conference as well as at the
University of Southern California. Hein would later
become a supervisor of officials in the American Football Conference.

Mel Hein and Phil Simms share the Giants record for
most seasons played with 15, but no Giant has ever
played in as many games as Hein did—172. The only
time in his career he came out of a game was when he
broke his nose in a game against the Brooklyn Dodgers
on Pearl Harbor day, 1941. That, however, proved to be
just a minor pit stop, as he would later return to action
in that game.

Mel Hein died on February 29, 1992, in San Clemente,
California. It is fair to say that in the history of the NFL,
no man played in as many minutes of game action as
Mel Hein did during his career—or ever will.

THE EARLY YEARS: 1925–55

Answers:

1. 1925.

2. d. The Providence Steam Roller.

3. The exact amount is not known, but accounts vary that the sum was between $500 and $2,500.

4. Mara was a bookmaker, which in 1925 was legal.

5. Tom Folwell.

6. Jim Thorpe.

7. Red Grange.

8. b. 1933—the Giants and the Chicago Bears met in the first NFL championship game played in Chicago. The Giants lost, 23–21.

9. The 1934 NFL championship game, when the Giants donned sneakers at halftime to best the Chicago Bears, 30–13, on the icy Polo Grounds turf.

10. a. 7—the Giants appeared in the NFL title game in 1933, 1934, 1935, 1938, 1939, 1941, and 1944.

11. Mel Hein.

12. Cal Hubbard. Hubbard was one of the great linemen in the 1920s and 1930s and later pursued a career as a major league umpire.

13. d. 2—the Giants beat the Chicago Bears in 1934 and the Detroit Lions in 1938.

14. Al Blozis.

15. c. Jack Lummus—Lummus, an end from Baylor, was awarded the Congressional Medal of Honor posthumously after serving with the Marines on Iwo Jima in 1945.

16. b. Jim Lee Howell.

17. c. Sid Luckman.

18. Steve Owen.

19. c. Alphonse "Tuffy" Leemans.

20. b. Ward Cuff.

21. Art Lewis, a tackle from Ohio University, played just one season with the Giants.

22. Ken Strong.

23. a. The Brooklyn Dodgers.

24. c. Steve Owen—the legendary head coach finished with 151 wins.

25. Emlen Tunnell, a defensive back from Iowa, would eventually be elected to the NFL Hall of Fame.

26. Quarterback Frank Filchock and fullback Merle Hapes. Both players declined the bribe, and Filchock turned in a gritty performance in the loss to the Bears. Filchock and Hapes opted to play in Canada following this incident but were later reinstated, (Filchock in 1954, Hapes in 1954), allowing them to finish their careers in the NFL.

27. True.

28. Charlie Conerly.

29. Vince Lombardi.

30. Conerly—Mississippi; Price—Tulane; Landry—Texas; Grier—Penn State; DeRogatis—Duke.

31. b. Bill Swiacki.

32. 1952.

33. Hap Moran, who took off for a 91-yard gallop against the Green Bay Packers in 1930.

34. a. Gene "Choo-Choo" Roberts.

35. Ben Agajanian.

36. a. The Los Angeles Rams.

37. Otto Schnellbacher.

38. Ben Agajanian.

39. Arnie Weinmeister.

40. b. Tom Landry.

41. Jim Lee Howell.

42. Alex Webster.

43. Roosevelt Grier.

44. Roosevelt Brown.

45. d. Kyle Rote.

2

THE GLORY YEARS: 1956–63

Questions:

1. Who was quarterback Charlie Conerly's backup from 1954 to 1959? a. Bobby Clatterbuck b. Don Heinrich c. Tom Dublinski d. George Shaw

2. Which Giants defender is held to have said, "We try to hurt everybody. We hit each other as hard as we can. This is a man's game"? a. Harland Svare b. Rosey Grier c. Sam Huff d. Andy Robustelli

3. How many touchdown passes did quarterback Y. A. Tittle throw in 1963? a. 29 b. 27 c. 41 d. 36

4. Who centered the Giants offensive line in the 1950s and early 1960s?

5. Which Baltimore Colt scored the winning touchdown in sudden death overtime in the 1958 NFL championship game against the Giants?

6. Who was the former Brooklyn College quarterback who later served as head coach of the Giants?

7. Which Giants kicker booted a 49-yard field goal in a snowstorm against the Cleveland Browns in 1958 to put the Giants in a playoff game against those same Browns for the Eastern Conference crown?

8. True or False: Quarterback Charlie Conerly never led the NFL in passing.

9. Who was known as the Chief? a. Phil King b. Don Chandler c. Frank Gifford d. Sam Huff

10. Name the two members of the Giants defense who attended tiny Arnold College in Connecticut.

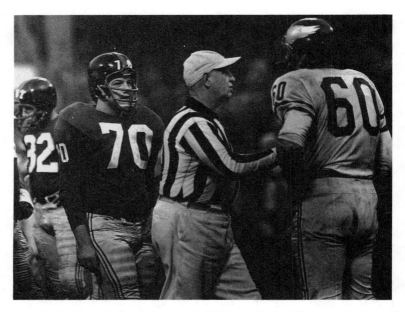

Sam Huff (70) and Chuck Bednarik (60), two Hall of Famers, square off in a Giants-Eagles tussle. (Dan Rubin)

11. Name the Eagles linebacker who knocked out Frank Gifford in a 1960 game, which led to Gifford retiring for one season.

12. Who scored the Giants' lone touchdown in the 1959 championship game rematch with the Baltimore Colts? a. Mel Triplett b. Bob Schnelker c. Phil King d. Joe Biscaha

13. Which Giants linebacker was the nemesis of the great Cleveland Browns running back Jim Brown?

14. Who did the Giants trade to the San Francisco 49ers in order to obtain quarterback Y. A. Tittle? a. Frank Youso b. Bob Simms c. Lou Cordileone d. Ed Sutton

15. Name the Brooklyn native and 1936 Olympic sprint hopeful who served as the radio voice of the Giants.

16. Who was known as Little Mo?

17. Name the rookie halfback who began his 14-year Giants career in 1959.

18. Name the Giants defensive back who scored three touchdowns on interception returns in 1963.

19. Who was Y. A. Tittle's favorite target from 1961 through 1963? a. Del Shofner b. Joe Walton c. Frank Gifford d. Paul Dudley

20. What was Y. A. Tittle's jersey number, which has been retired?

21. Who was the Giants kicker who handled both the punting and placekicking from 1962 through 1964?

22. What was the score of the 1958 sudden death overtime championship game between the Giants and the Baltimore Colts? a. 23–16 b. 24–17 c. 26–20 d. 23–17

23. What was the score of the 1959 Giants–Baltimore Colts NFL championship game? a. 40–17 b. 35–12 c. 31–16 d. 24–13

24. Match the player with his alma mater:

Sam Huff	LSU
Del Shofner	Notre Dame
Dick Lynch	Baylor
Joe Walton	West Virginia
Y. A. Tittle	Pittsburgh

25. Name the clubhouse man who designed the play that worked for a touchdown in the crucial game against the Eagles in 1961.

26. What was the nature of Y. A. Tittle's injury in the 1963 NFL championship game? a. Groin pull b. Sprained knee c. Concussion d. Separated shoulder

27. Which Eastern Division foe did the Giants humiliate 53–0 in a 1961 game at Yankee Stadium? a. The Los Angeles Rams b. The Detroit Lions c. The San Francisco 49ers d. The Washington Redskins

28. Who was the sure-handed, undersized tight end of the Y. A. Tittle years? a. Joe Walton b. Del Shofner c. Lee Grosscup d. Allan Webb

Y. A. Tittle (14) in action against the Pittsburgh Steelers. (Dan Rubin)

29. Who was the halfback who wore number 13 for the Giants and wore the same number as a New York Titans and New York Jets receiver?

30. Name the University of Utah quarterback who was a first-round draft pick in 1959 but had a short career in the NFL.

31. Which Giants defensive back went 102 yards for a touchdown with an interception return against the Dallas Cowboys in a 1961 game? a. Carl "Spider" Lockhart b. Erich Barnes c. Dick Nolan d. Jimmy Patton

32. Name the Giant who scored the lone touchdown for the team in the championship title game losses to the Green Bay Packers in both 1961 and 1962. a. Sam Horner b. Johnny Counts c. Jim Collier d. Alex Webster

33. Who was the rookie quarterback who replaced Y. A. Tittle after Tittle went down with an injury in the 1963 title game against the Chicago Bears?

34. Who was the first Giant to gain more than 1,000 yards on pass receptions? a. Del Shofner b. Homer Jones c. Frank Gifford d. Kyle Rote

35. Name the quarterback who replaced the oft-injured Charlie Conerly during the 1960 season.

36. Which Eastern Conference foe introduced the safety blitz to upset the Giants in the 1961 season opener, 21–10? a. The Dallas Cowboys b. The St. Louis Cardinals c. The Cleveland Browns d. The Washington Redskins

37. How many times did Y. A. Tittle throw seven touchdown passes in a game, tying an NFL record? a. Three times b. Two times c. Five times d. Once

38. Which Giants running back had a big comeback year in 1961, leading the team in rushing? a. Frank Gifford b. Alex Webster c. Joel Wells d. Bob Gaiters

39. What was the final score of the 1961 championship game against the Green Bay Packers?

40. In which round was Joe Morrison drafted in the 1959 NFL draft?

41. Which Giant appeared on the cover of *Time* magazine in November 1959? a. Sam Huff b. Frank Gifford c. Charley Conerly d. Rosey Grier

42. Name the former San Francisco 49er and Hall of Fame running back the Giants picked up prior to the start of the 1963 season.

43. Which Brooklyn high school did Giants head coach Allie Sherman attend? a. Brooklyn Tech b. Boys High School c. Canarsie High School d. Erasmus Hall High School

44. Which team did the Giants play the weekend of President Kennedy's assassination? a. The Baltimore Colts b. The Dallas Cowboys c. The St. Louis Cardinals d. The Washington Redskins

45. How many 300-yard passing games did Y. A. Tittle have during the 1962 season? a. 4 b. 6 c. 7 d. 1

Giants defense in action in 1961 game against the Cardinals. (Dan Rubin)

46. Name the Giants linebacker from the late 1950s who later became an NFL head coach.

47. Who is the Giants all-time leading pass receiver, with 395 catches? a. Del Shofner b. Kyle Rote c. Joe Morrison d. Frank Gifford

48. How many championship games did Frank Gifford play in? a. 7 b. 3 c. 6 d. 5

49. Match the player with his alma mater:

Dick Modzelewski	Purdue
Jack Stroud	UCLA
Bill Stits	Tennessee
Phil King	Maryland
Erich Barnes	Vanderbilt

50. Who was defensive tackle Rosey Grier traded to the Los Angeles Rams for in 1963? a. Jim Moran b. John Lovetere c. Stan Fanning d. Lamar Lundy

51. Which year did the Giants move from the Polo Grounds to Yankee Stadium? a. 1957 b. 1956 c. 1961 d. 1959

52. Which year was Frank Gifford voted the NFL Player of the Year? a. 1958 b. 1960 c. 1959 d. 1956

53. Which team did the Giants beat for the 1956 NFL title? a. The Chicago Bears b. The Chicago Cardinals c. The Cleveland Browns d. The San Francisco 49ers

54. Name the two Giants running backs who scored touchdowns in the 1956 championship game against the Chicago Bears.

55. What was Frank Gifford's jersey number?

The Giant with a Heart

Emlen Tunnell. (New York Giants)

It was 1948, the year after Jackie Robinson first stepped up to the plate at Ebbets Field in Brooklyn, breaking the color barrier in major league baseball, when Emlen Tunnell walked into the Giants offices and asked for a tryout. Emlen Tunnell was granted his tryout—and lucky for the Giants, who found themselves a star. Emlen Tunnell found himself on an NFL roster and in doing so became the first African American to play for the New York Giants.

Tunnell played for the Giants from 1948 through 1958 in head coach Steve Owen's Umbrella Defense. He played alongside such stars as Otto Schnellbacher, Harmon Rowe, and Tom Landry in the Giants secondary and holds the team record for career interceptions with 74, as well as many team punt-return records.

At the time of Emlen Tunnell's death at the still young age of 50 he was the Giants assistant director of player personnel. He also served as a scout and assistant coach. Despite his exploits on the field he was best remembered by his teammates as a caring and compassionate man.

"He was good to all people. He was a hell of a decent person," teammate Andy Robustelli said of Tunnell. No story, though, illustrates this better than the "day" the Giants celebrated for Tunnell in his final season with them in 1958. On his way to the stadium, Tunnell was stopped by a number of men standing outside the entrance to Yankee Stadium who gave him what he would consider the most touching gift he would receive that day. They were homeless men who had passed the hat around for their friend who had never forgotten them. They raised $28.

"It was the best gift," he later explained, "because if they had a million bucks, they'd have given it to me. They were guys who hung around the ballpark, guys I'd given a dime or quarter to when I started playing at the Polo Grounds, and then they hung around Yankee Stadium when the Giants moved there."

Emlen Tunnell capped his illustrious career in the pros by being the first African American to be named an assistant coach in the NFL. He was the Giants defensive backfield coach in the mid-1960s. In 1967 he achieved another first—the first African American inducted into the pro football Hall of Fame.

Big Rosey

During his 12-year NFL career, spanning the years from 1955 to 1967, Roosevelt Grier was considered one of the most formidable defensive tackles in the league. The six-foot-five-inch, 300-pound Grier played on five Eastern Conference championship teams as well as on the 1956 Giants team that beat the Chicago Bears, 47–7, to win the NFL title. He was named to the All-Pro team that season.

In 1963, Roosevelt Grier was traded to the Los Angeles Rams for defensive tackle John Lovetere, and for the next five seasons Grier became a vital cog in the Rams' Fearsome Foursome defensive line that featured Hall of Famers David "Deacon" Jones, Merlin Olsen, and Lamar Lundy.

Though bitter and angry at his trade to the Rams, Grier settled into the L.A. scene and began to pursue his other passions, music and acting. He appeared and sang on many television variety shows and recorded a couple of songs. Grier also acted on several television series, including *The Man from U.N.C.L.E., Daniel Boone,* and *Mr. Novak,* but Grier soon proved to be a man of other callings.

Among teammates Grier was known for his kindness and compassion. He admitted that one of his biggest fears as a player was that he could injure an opponent. In the years following his retirement from the game, Grier has tried to make the world a better place through his many acts of kindness. He has been a political activist, best remembered as Robert F. Kennedy's bodyguard that tragic night in Los Angeles in 1968 when Kennedy was assassinated by Sirhan Sirhan. It was Grier who wrestled the pistol away from Sirhan after the fatal shots were fired. "He killed my dream," Grier recently said in an interview when asked about that sorrowful night.

This gentle giant has been a devotee of needlepoint. "I get keyed up a lot, you know, and I can sit and do something like this and kind of get away from it all," he once said about his hobby. Grier even published a book in 1973 about his relaxing passion, *Rosey Grier's Needlepoint for Men.*

Roosevelt Grier is now a minister. He has worked for the Special Olympics and has headed literacy programs in Los Angeles. Roosevelt Grier has also visited O. J. Simpson in the Los Angeles County Jail. Wherever Grier has gone he continues to preach his gospel of compassion, brotherhood, and love.

Plugged-in Giants

Paul Brown was considered one of the most innovative coaches in the history of the NFL. Brown was responsible for such breakthroughs as the playbook, the face mask, and the draw play, and he was the first head coach to place his assistant coaches in the press box complete with phones to contact the sidelines during the game. In 1956, Paul Brown might have even outdone himself when he decided to put a radio receiver in his quarterback's helmet. During the course of the game Brown would transmit plays to his quarterback through a hand mike.

The Giants began the 1956 season on the road at Cleveland. They were prepared for the Browns' electronic gadgetry. Bob Topp, a former Michigan end who was on the Giants payroll, operated a radio receiver on the Giants bench and picked up Paul Brown's instructions to his quarterback, George Ratterman. Gene Filipski, a halfback the Giants acquired from Cleveland several weeks earlier, was held in readiness in the event Brown went with a number system to call his plays.

Once the game started Topp relayed the Browns' instructions to Tom Landry, the Giants defensive coach, who would then shout the Cleveland offensive plays to his players on the field. Throughout the game the Giants stymied the Cleveland offense.

After the game Paul Brown complained that due to crowd noises he used the radio only on the first series of downs. The Giants' 21–9 victory that day was their first triumph over the Browns in three seasons. Several other teams also tried electronic devices to send plays into games, but by midseason NFL commissioner Bert Bell ordered a league-wide ban on all electronic gadgetry.

The Apprenticeship of Vince and Tom

Before Vince Lombardi went to Green Bay and became an NFL icon and before Tom Landry headed down to Dallas to become the fabled "man in the hat," they learned the pro coaching trade as assistant coaches in the 1950s with the Giants under Jim Lee Howell.

Vince Lombardi was recruited from the Army coaching staff, where he served under the legendary Army head coach Earl "Red" Blaik as the backfield coach. He left West Point in 1954 to become the Giants offensive coach. "Vince Lombardi," Frank Gifford has said, "is responsible for my success." Prior to Lombardi's arrival with the Giants, Gifford had played cornerback and safety as well as seeing spot duty on offense. Lombardi told Gifford on the first day of training camp in 1954 that he was his halfback. Gifford later admitted that Lombardi's faith in him was a confidence builder. During his tenure as the Giants offensive coach from 1954 through 1958, Vince Lombardi revamped and ran the offense for Jim Lee Howell.

Though he was one of Fordham University's famed Seven Blocks of Granite in the 1930s and a classmate of Giants owner Wellington Mara, Lombardi never played professional football. Instead, while he was with the Giants, Vince Lombardi learned the pro game and sharpened his coaching techniques. What Lombardi learned while with the Giants proved invaluable at Green Bay, as Lombardi was laying the foundation for the Packers dynasty of the 1960s, when Green Bay would go on to win five league titles.

While Vince Lombardi ran the offense, Tom Landry ran the defense. The former University of Texas quarterback was picked up from the old All-American Football Conference in 1950 and served the Giants well as both a defensive back and defensive coach before he left to become the first head coach for the Dallas Cowboys, in 1960. Teammate Frank Gifford said Landry

29

Head-to-head collision: The Tom Landry–coached defense in action in 1959 battle with the Browns as Sam Huff (70) sticks it to Jim Brown. (Dan Rubin)

had a knack of knowing what plays the offense would call. In 1954, Landry assumed the dual role of player and defensive coach.

Landry wore those two hats during the 1954 and 1955 seasons, and in 1955, after his final season as a player, he became solely the team's defensive coach. Landry is credited as having been the innovator of the 4–3 defense, and in an era before computers and video, he broke down the opponents' films and studied their offense, looking for tendencies. During Landry's coaching tenure from 1954 through 1959, the Giants played in three NFL championship games.

Though he once admitted that he never had any ambition to be a head coach, Tom Landry left the Giants in 1960 to lead the Dallas Cowboys in their maiden season in the NFL. Tom Landry put together a string of 20 consecutive winning seasons and two Super Bowl triumphs during his 29 years as head coach of the Cowboys. It is fair to say Tom Landry and Vince Lombardi gained invaluable experience during coaching apprenticeships with the Giants long before their great head-coaching talents were exposed.

"The Best Football Game Ever Played"

After beating the Cleveland Browns in a 1958 conference playoff game, 10–0, the Giants won the right to fight it out with the Baltimore Colts for the NFL championship on December 28 at Yankee Stadium.

The 1958 Colts would place five of its members in the Hall of Fame: quarterback Johnny Unitas, halfback Lenny Moore, wide receiver Raymond Berry, offensive tackle Jim Parker, and defensive end Gino Marchetti. They had a record identical to the Giants' for the season: nine wins and three losses.

Sixty-four thousand fans huddled into Yankee Stadium on that cold December afternoon. Due to television contracts with the NFL at the time, the game was blacked out in the New York area. At the same time a newspaper strike crippled news-starved New Yorkers, thus making it impossible for them to read about the game.

The Giants drew first blood as Pat Summerall accounted for all the first-quarter scoring himself, nailing a 36-yard field goal. The second quarter, though, belonged to the Colts, who threatened to blow the Giants out of Yankee Stadium. Their fullback, Alan Ameche, carried the ball in from two yards out for the first Colts touchdown, and later that period Johnny Unitas hit Raymond Berry in the end zone with a 15-yard strike, giving Baltimore a 14–3 halftime lead.

A goal-line stand sparked the Giants in the third quarter. New York moved the ball smartly downfield, the key play on the drive being a long pass from quarterback Charlie Conerly to Kyle Rote, who hauled it in and took it down to the Colts 25-yard line. Only one glitch on the play: Rote left the ball on the ground. Luckily, Johnny-on-the-spot teammate Alex Webster recovered the fumble and headed for the Colts end zone before being tackled on the one-yard line. Mel Triplett took it in on

Alan Ameche ends "The Best Football Game Ever Played" as he crosses the goal line in sudden-death overtime in the 1958 NFL championship game. (AP/Wide World Photos)

the next play, and the Giants were back in the game, having cut the Colts lead to 14–10.

In the fourth quarter, with the Colts still clinging to their four-point lead, the Giants struck again. Conerly hit Frank Gifford with a 15-yard touchdown pass, and suddenly the Giants had their first lead since the first quarter, 17–14. Visions of an NFL title floated through the minds of the Giants faithful. However, a legend—and history—was about to be made.

With two minutes to go in the game, the Colts took possession of the ball on their own 14-yard line. Johnny Unitas coolly picked apart the Giants defense, moving Baltimore downfield to the Giants 13-yard line with seven seconds to play. Steve Myra was called on by Baltimore coach Weeb Ewbank to tie the game. When he booted a 27-yard field goal, evening the score at 17–all, he forced the first-ever sudden death overtime game in NFL championship game history.

In the overtime the Giants took the ball first but were

halted by the Colts defense. Following a Don Chandler punt, Baltimore took over the ball on their own 20-yard line. Once again Johnny Unitas coolly led his team down the field. The drive, and the game, culminated as Alan Ameche bulled across the goal line from the two-yard line, giving Baltimore the NFL championship, 23–17.

Millions of fans across America watched the sudden death game. The Giants-Colts battle caught the imagination of the nation, and the television industry realized that it had a gem in covering pro football. In the January 5, 1959, issue of *Sports Illustrated,* writer Tex Maule, who covered the game, headlined his piece, THE BEST FOOTBALL GAME EVER PLAYED.

Close but No Cigar

From 1958 through 1963 the Giants appeared in five NFL championship games, but the football gods didn't smile on the boys from the Big Apple. The sad stories are as follows.

1958: The Baltimore Colts beat the Giants in sudden death overtime, 23–17, at Yankee Stadium, the game just described.

1959: In a rematch of their 1958 overtime classic, this time in Baltimore, the Giants took a 9–7 lead into the fourth quarter, but the Colts exploded for 24 points as Johnny Unitas ran for a touchdown, threw for another, and Johnny Sample picked off a Charlie Conerly pass and ran it back for yet another Colts score as Baltimore beat the Giants, 31–16.

1961: The Giants traveled to frigid Green Bay, Wisconsin, to take on Vince Lombardi's Packers. The Packers and the arctic conditions hampered the Giants passing attack as Y. A. Tittle and Charlie Conerly threw for only 119 yards between them, and the Giants suffered their most humiliating defeat in a title game, 37–0.

1962: The Giants sought revenge for their embarrassing 1961 title game loss to Green Bay in the rematch against Vince Lombardi's powerful 13–1 Packers at Yankee Stadium. Again the Giants were facing arctic conditions—and they weren't even in Green Bay this time—as 40-mile-per-hour winds and a wind chill factor of nearly zero virtually nullified Y. A. Tittle's pass-oriented offense. The game turned into a brutal smash-mouth contest in which Green Bay fullback Jim Taylor and Giants middle linebacker Sam Huff fought a violent battle with one another throughout the game. At one point Taylor, following a vicious Huff hit, swallowed his tongue. At the final gun, however, the Giants were bested again, 16–7.

1963: During the regular season Y. A. Tittle threw for a Giants season record 36 touchdown passes, and the G-men placed eight players on the Pro Bowl team,

1962 NFL championship game at Yankee Stadium: Giants vs. Packers. (Dan Rubin)

finishing 11–3. They squared off against the Chicago Bears in the championship game December 29 at Wrigley Field in Chicago.

The Giants once again faced weather conditions that hampered their pass-oriented offense with high winds, nine-degree temperatures, and a knee injury to Tittle. The Bears held on for a 14–10 win and the NFL championship.

The bitter loss to the Bears that day ended the Giants' Glory Years, as the team would begin an 18-year descent into NFL wasteland, wandering about the NFL desert until 1981, when they would reward their devoutly loyal fans with a playoff berth.

THE GLORY YEARS: 1956–63

Answers:

1. b. Don Heinrich.

2. c. Sam Huff.

3. d. 36—still a Giants single-season record for most touchdown passes.

4. Ray Wietecha.

5. Alan Ameche.

6. Allie Sherman.

7. Pat Summerall.

8. False—Charlie Conerly led the NFL in passing in 1959.

9. a. Phil King.

10. Andy Robustelli and Alan Webb.

11. Chuck Bednarik.

12. b. Bob Schnelker.

13. Sam Huff.

14. c. Guard Lou Cordileone.

15. Marty Glickman.

16. Defensive tackle Dick Modzelewski.

17. Joe Morrison.

18. Dick Lynch.

19. a. Del Shofner.

20. #14.

21. Don Chandler.

22. d. The Colts won 23–17.

23. c. The Colts won again, 31–16.

24. Huff—West Virginia; Shofner—Baylor; Lynch—Notre Dame; Walton—Pittsburgh; Tittle—LSU.

25. Pete Previte.

26. b. Tittle suffered a sprained knee.

27. d. The Washington Redskins.

28. a. Joe Walton.

29. Don Maynard.

30. Lee Grosscup.

31. b. Erich Barnes.

32. c. Jim Collier.

33. Glynn Griffing.

34. a. Del Shofner.

35. George Shaw.

36. b. The St. Louis Cardinals.

37. d. Only once.

38. b. Alex Webster.

39. Green Bay won 37–0.

40. The third.

41. a. Sam Huff.

42. Hugh McElhenny.

43. b. Boys High School.

44. c. The St. Louis Cardinals.

45. a. Four.

46. Harland Svare.

47. c. Joe Morrison, with 395 receptions.

48. d. Five.

49. Modzelewski—Maryland; Stroud—Tennessee; Stits—UCLA; King—Vanderbilt; Barnes—Purdue.

50. b. John Lovetere.

51. b. 1956.

52. d. 1956.

53. a. The Chicago Bears.

54. Mel Triplett and Alex Webster.

55. #16.

3

Wandering in the Gridiron Desert: 1964–80

Questions:

1. The Giants recorded their worst record when they finished 1–12–1. What season did that take place? a. 1983 b. 1973 c. 1966 d. 1980

2. Which team was Sam Huff traded to? a. The Detroit Lions b. The Washington Redskins c. The Chicago Bears d. The Pittsburgh Steelers

3. Name the Cornell University quarterback who spelled Y. A. Tittle in Tittle's final season.

4. What year did both Frank Gifford and Alex Webster retire? a. 1964 b. 1965 c. 1963 d. 1967

5. True or False: Tucker Frederickson was the NFL rookie of the year in 1965.

6. Name the tackle from the University of Missouri taken by the Giants in the first round of the 1966 draft.

7. Who was the quarterback who helped guide the Giants to a 7–7 record in 1965 and would later share quarterback duties with Bob Griese during the Miami Dolphins' perfect 17–0 season in 1972? a. Earl Morrall b. Norm Snead c. George Mira d. Milt Plum

8. Who was the first Giants running back to rush for more than 1,000 yards in a season? a. Joe Morris b. Frank Gifford c. Joe Morrison d. Ron Johnson

9. Who won, and what was the final score, of the first Giants-Jets regular season game? a. Giants, 31–13 b. Jets, 21–20 c. Giants, 17–10 d. Giants, 22–10

Tucker Frederickson. (New York Giants)

10. Name the Hungarian soccer-style kicker the Giants picked up from the Buffalo Bills in 1964.

11. Name the gritty tackle from Grambling University who played in the middle of the Giants defensive line in the 1970s.

12. The Giants traded quarterback Fran Tarkenton back to the Minnesota Vikings for which veteran quarterback? a. John Hadl b. Jack Concannon c. Norm Snead d. Frank Ryan

13. Name the sure-handed receiver who was also acquired by the Giants from Minnesota in the Fran Tarkenton deal.

14. The NFL record for total points in a single game was set in the Giants' 72–41 loss to which team? a. The Philadelphia Eagles b. The Washington Redskins c. The Baltimore Colts d. The Cleveland Browns

15. Name the bizarre-acting running back the Giants took in the first round of the NFL draft and later traded to the Baltimore Colts in 1964.

16. Which former Giants star became head football coach at the University of South Carolina?

17. Who was the speedster from Texas Southern University who holds the record for the longest Giants touchdown reception? a. Coleman Zeno b. Rocky Thompson c. Earnest Gray d. Homer Jones

18. Which season was the first for the Giants to call the Meadowlands home? a. 1976 b. 1977 c. 1975 d. 1974

19. What was the final score of the first game played by the Giants at Giants Stadium in the Meadowlands?

20. Who scored the first touchdown by the Giants at the Meadlowlands? a. Jimmy Robinson b. Doug Kotar c. Craig Morton d. Larry Csonka

21. How many seasons did Fran Tarkenton play for the Giants? a. 3 b. 5 c. 6 d. 4

22. Who replaced Allie Sherman as Giants coach in 1969?

23. Name the wiry, skillful safety who played with the Giants from 1965 to 1975 and had 41 career interceptions.

24. How many 1,000-yard-rushing seasons did Ron Johnson have?

25. Who was the Philadelphia Eagles defender who scored a touchdown after the fumbled handoff between Joe Pisarcik and Larry Csonka in the infamous 1978 game at the Meadowlands?

Alex Webster served the Giants as player and coach. (New York Giants)

26. What year was linebacker Harry Carson drafted?

27. Which team was Homer Jones traded to in 1970? a. The New Orleans Saints b. The Atlanta Falcons c. The Cleveland Browns ˙d. The Buffalo Bills

28. The Giants, and Giants fans, were expecting big things from the 1973 Giants team that went 6–0 in the preseason but were sadly disappointed once the regular season began. What was the Giants' record during the regular season that year?

29. Who coached the Giants from 1976 to 1978?

30. Who was the solid defensive tackle and first-round draft pick from Colorado who was killed in an auto accident in 1979?

31. Which Giant led the NFC in receiving in 1971? a. Bob Tucker b. Rich Houston c. Dick Kotite d. Junior Coffey

32. How many seasons did Larry Csonka play for the Giants?

33. What former Giant quarterbacked the Denver Broncos to a surprising appearance in Super Bowl XII?

34. What was the NFC-leading number of passes caught in 1971? a. 61 b. 59 c. 70 d. 64

35. Who was the Michigan State University safety who chose professional football over baseball and had an outstanding career as a Giants linebacker from 1973 to 1983?

36. Match the player with his alma mater:

Ron Johnson	North Texas State
Bob Tucker	Cal Lutheran
Carl Lockhart	South Carolina State
Harry Carson	Bloomsburg State
Brian Kelley	Michigan

37. Who did Joe Pisarcik play for before joining the Giants? a. The Philadelphia Eagles b. The New York Stars (World Football League) c. The Calgary Stampeders d. The Bridgeport Jets (East Coast Football League)

38. Who did the Giants play and what was the final score of the Giants' last game at Yankee Stadium on September 23, 1973? a. Dallas 27, Giants 21 b. Giants 14, St. Louis 7 c. Giants 16, Baltimore 13 d. Giants 23, Philadelphia 23

39. Name the team the Giants had to beat in the final game of the 1970 season to qualify for the playoffs and the final score.

40. Name the Ohio State University Buckeye who as a rookie in 1964 was drafted by both the Giants and the Jets and which team he chose to play with.

41. Name the free-spirited Giants defensive end from San Diego State University who has been a leading man on television and in film.

42. Who was the slashing Giants running back from the University of Kentucky who led the team in rushing in 1976 and 1978 and died of cancer in 1983?

43. Who was the solid veteran pass-rushing defensive end the Giants picked up from the Cleveland Browns before the 1972 season? a. Charlie Harper b. Dan Goich c. Jack Gregory d. Pat Hughes

44. Who was the tight end for the Giants in the late 1960s and early 1970s who has served as an NFL head coach? a. Tom Gatewood b. Rich Kotite c. Bob Tucker d. Bob Crespino

45. Giants draftniks booed the team's first-round draft pick in 1979, a quarterback who led a small college to a 2–6–1 record the year before. Who was that pick?

46. Which year did George Young become the Giants general manager? a. 1980 b. 1977 c. 1981 d. 1979

47. True or False: Before the Giants beat the Redskins 12–9 in a 1976 game at Giants Stadium, the Redskins had a 12-game winning streak against New York.

48. What job did Ray Perkins hold before he was named as Giants head coach in 1979?

49. How many touchdown passes did Phil Simms throw in his rookie season of 1979? a. 13 b. 16 c. 14 d. 9

50. Who led the Giants in receiving in 1979—most of the passes being thrown by fellow Morehead State alumnus Phil Simms?

51. True or False: The Giants shut down O. J. Simpson on a Monday night game in 1975.

Carl "Spider" Lockhart, a tough, smart safety during the Giants' lean years. (New York Giants)

52. Which team did George Young come over from to be Giants general manager? a. The San Diego Chargers b. The Tampa Bay Buccaneers c. The Miami Dolphins d. The Oakland Raiders

53. Name the Giants player credited with inventing the spike.

54. Which pro football team did Ray Perkins play for? a. The Kansas City Chiefs b. The Baltimore Colts c. The Denver Broncos d. The Boston Patriots

55. Name the Giants wide receiver who caught four touchdown passes in a 1980 game against the St. Louis Cardinals.

56. When the Giants moved into Giants Stadium in 1976, that became their fifth home stadium. Name the other four.

57. Which Giants running back led the team in rushing in 1979 and is now a sportscaster? a. Billy Taylor b. Emery Moorehead c. Bobby Hammond d. Bo Matthews

The Saga of
Joe Don Looney

Even though Joe Don Looney was tossed off the University of Oklahoma football team three games into his senior season for fighting with an assistant coach, the Giants made him their number one pick in the NFL draft for the 1964 season.

The Giants were intrigued by the former Sooners running back's size and speed. Looney packed 230 rock-solid pounds on a six-foot-two-inch frame and could run the hundred-yard dash in 9.5 seconds. Difficulties, though, soon arose when Joe Don reported to the Giants training camp at Fairfield, Connecticut, in the summer of 1964.

Refusing to speak to reporters, Looney told them he was in training camp to play football, not to talk, and though he displayed unusual speed for a man his size, there were other problems in dealing with Joe Don. Looney refused to attend team meetings, skipped a number of practices, and was fined numerous times for refusing to have his ankles taped. He also balked at having the team trainer look at his leg after he pulled a muscle, telling head coach Allie Sherman, "It's my leg, not the trainer's." Y. A. Tittle reached out to Looney and asked him if he would like to attend a pregame meeting before an exhibition game. Looney declined, saying, "I don't know, Y. A., I gotta rest up." After 28 days in training camp, the Giants traded Looney to the Baltimore Colts.

Joe Don Looney bounced from Baltimore to Washington to Detroit to New Orleans, with an army stint in Vietnam thrown in along the way. He maintained his noncomformist ways and never stayed with any of those clubs for too long.

Certainly, Joe Don Looney never lived up to the enormous football greatness many had predicted for him. Rather, years of drug addiction and, later, enchantment with Eastern religion dominated Looney's life. He fol-

Enigmatic Joe Don Looney: a haunting legacy of unfulfilled potential. (University of Oklahoma)

lowed his guru, Swami Baba Muktananda, to India, where he tended his guru's elephant.

After time, though, Looney grew disenchanted with Baba Muktananda and returned to the United States, settling in his native Texas. Joe Don Looney was killed in a motorcycle accident near his Texas home in 1988. He was 45 years old.

The First Spiker

Homer Jones, en route to the end zone—and a spike! (Dan Rubin)

Homer Jones played flanker for the Giants from 1964 through 1969. He was a sturdily built man who sometimes ran pass patterns that weren't in the playbook. Quarterback Earl Morrall once said that Jones was so fast he could outrun a 70-yard pass.

Homer Jones finished his NFL career with the Cleveland Browns in 1970, but Jones is best remembered as a Giant. He is in the Giants record book for most touchdown passes caught in a season: 13 in 1967; longest reception for a touchdown: 98 yards against the Steelers in 1966; highest average per catch for a season: 24.7 yards in 1967; highest average per catch for a career: 22.6 yards on 214 career receptions; and also most yards receiving in a season: 1,209 in 1967. But Homer

Jones is also remembered by some as the NFL's first spiker.

Homer Jones promised that when he scored his first touchdown in the NFL he would throw the ball up into the stands. However, he also remembered the league rule that there was a $500 fine for such a celebration.

Jones recalled that when he crossed the goal line in a crucial game in the mid-1960s, instead of throwing the ball into the stands and having the fine levied against him by the league, he threw the ball on the ground emphatically, and the spike was born.

Wandering in the Gridiron Desert: 1964–80

Answers:

1. c. 1966.

2. b. The Washington Redskins.

3. Gary Wood.

4. a. At the end of the 1964 season.

5. False—it was Gale Sayers of the Chicago Bears.

6. Francis Peay.

7. a. Earl Morrall.

8. d. Ron Johnson.

9. d. The Giants, 22–10, in a 1970 game at Shea Stadium.

10. Pete Gogolak.

11. John Mendenhall.

12. c. Norm Snead.

13. Bob Grim.

14. b. The Washington Redskins.

15. Joe Don Looney.

16. Joe Morrison.

17. d. Homer Jones had a 98-yard reception against the Pittsburgh Steelers in 1966.

18. a. 1976.

19. The Giants lost to the Dallas Cowboys 24–14 on October 10, 1976.

20. a. Jimmy Robinson on a pass from Craig Morton against the Dallas Cowboys.

21. b. Five, 1967–71.

22. Alex Webster.

23. Carl Lockhart.

24. Two.

25. Herman Edwards.

26. 1976.

27. c. The Cleveland Browns.

28. 2–11–1.

29. John McVay.

30. Troy Archer.

31. a. Bob Tucker.

32. Three seasons, 1976–78.

33. Craig Morton.

34. b. 59.

35. Brad Van Pelt.

36. Johnson—Michigan; Tucker—Bloomsburg State; Lockhart—North Texas State; Carson—South Carolina State; Kelley—Cal Lutheran.

37. c. The Calgary Stampeders of the Canadian Football League.

38. d. The Giants and Eagles tied at 23-all.

39. The Los Angeles Rams, who beat the Giants 31–3.

40. Matt Snell—the Jets.

41. Fred Dryer.

42. Doug Kotar.

43. c. Jack Gregory.

44. b. Rich Kotite.

45. Phil Simms.

46. d. 1979.

47. True.

48. Ray Perkins was the offensive coordinator for the San Diego Chargers.

49. a. 13.

50. Gary Shirk.

51. Simpson managed his yards in that game—128 yards rushing—but the Giants won the game over the previously undefeated Buffalo Bills.

52. George Young was director of player personnel for the Miami Dolphins.

53. Homer Jones.

54. b. Ray Perkins was a wide receiver for the Baltimore Colts from 1967 to 1971.

55. Earnest Gray.

56. The Polo Grounds, Yankee Stadium, the Yale Bowl, and Shea Stadium.

57. a. Billy Taylor.

4

REBIRTH AND TRIUMPH: 1981–90

Questions:

1. Who was the powerful running back the Giants picked up from the Houston Oilers during the 1981 season?

2. True or False: Bill Parcells was once an assistant coach at Navy.

3. Which season was Lawrence Taylor's rookie season?

4. Name the player selected ahead of Lawrence Taylor in the NFL draft.

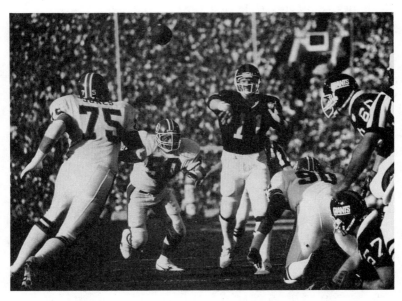

Phil Simms leads the way for the Giants in their Super Bowl XXI win over Denver. (Jerry Pinkus)

5. Which Giants kicker made the overtime field goal in the final regular season game against the Dallas Cowboys to help put the Giants in the 1981 playoffs—their first playoff appearance in eighteen years? a. Ali Haji-Sheikh b. Joe Danelo c. Dave Jennings d. Eric Schubert

6. For which college team did Ray Perkins leave the Giants toward the end of the 1982 season to become head coach? a. Auburn b. Tennessee c. Purdue d. Alabama

7. Which Giants linebacker picked off a Danny White pass in sudden death overtime in the 1981 season finale against the Dallas Cowboys that helped set up the winning field goal? a. Brad Van Pelt b. Lawrence Taylor c. Byron Hunt d. Harry Carson

8. In 1981, when the Giants qualified for their first playoff game in 18 years, they played the Philadelphia Eagles in an NFC wild card game. What was the final score? a. Eagles 36, Giants 20 b. Giants 27, Eagles 21 c. Giants 17, Eagles 10 d. Giants 16, Eagles 13 in overtime

9. Which year did Phil Simms pass for a Giants team record 4,004 yards? a. 1986 b. 1985 c. 1989 d. 1984

10. Match the player with his alma mater:

Joe Morris	Oregon
Mark Bavaro	Michigan State
George Martin	Syracuse
Carl Banks	Iowa State
Karl Nelson	Notre Dame

11. Who said, "Once a Giant, always a Giant, that's loyalty that remains." a. Pat Summerall b. Frank Gifford c. Allie Sherman d. Fran Tarkenton

12. Who was the quarterback chosen by Bill Parcells as the Giants starting quarterback over Phil Simms in Parcells's first season as head coach?

13. What was linebacking great Harry Carson's jersey number?

14. Which Giant holds the record for most touchdowns scored by a defensive lineman?

15. Which team did Brad Van Pelt join after he left the Giants? a. The Houston Oilers b. The New England Patriots c. The Los Angeles Raiders d. The Los Angeles Rams

16. In a 1982 Thanksgiving Day game, Lawrence Taylor scored a 97-yard touchdown against which team?

17. Name the blocking back who cleared the way for Joe Morris.

18. Which season was the first in which Joe Morris gained 1,000 yards rushing? a. 1985 b. 1988 c. 1984 d. 1986

19. Who was the tight end for the Giants who scored their first touchdown in Super Bowl XXI against the Denver Broncos?

20. Who was the All-Pro cornerback from the University of Colorado traded by the Giants to the Denver Broncos in 1986?

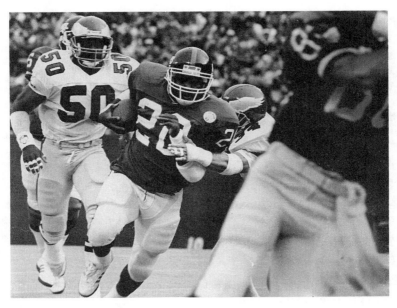

Joe Morris eludes Eagles defenders and heads upfield. (Jerry Pinkus)

21. Who was the Giants receiver who caught a crucial fourth-down-and-18-yards-to-go pass against the Minnesota Vikings in a key 1986 game leading to a Giants victory? a. Phil McConkey b. Stacy Robinson c. Lionel Manuel d. Bobby Johnson

22. Name the placekicker released by the Giants but then called back by the team for a 1985 game against the Tampa Bay Buccaneers—a game in which he kicked five field goals.

23. What is the Giants record for pass completions in a game? a. 37 by Phil Simms in 1989 b. 40 by Phil Simms in 1985 c. 42 by Scott Brunner in 1983 d. 39 by Jeff Hostetler in 1990

24. Name the Giants nose tackle who knocked Joe Montana out of the 1986 playoff game between the Giants and the San Francisco 49ers.

25. Who was the running back who went into the offensive huddle on third downs during the championship season of 1986? a. Lee Rouson b. Ottis Anderson c. Tony Galbreath d. Rob Carpenter

26. What was the final score of the Giants–Washington Redskins NFC championship game in January 1987? a. Giants 23, Washington 3 b. Giants 30, Washington 3 c. Giants 20, Washington 10 d. Giants 17, Washington 0

27. Name the gutsy Giants receiver who caught a touchdown pass in Super Bowl XXI against the Denver Broncos when the ball bounced off tight end Mark Bavaro's hands in the end zone.

28. Which Giants running back carried the ball 43 times in a game against the Tampa Bay Buccaneers in 1983? a. Joe Morris b. Butch Woolfolk c. Rob Carpenter d. George Adams

29. Which Giant set a team record for touchdowns in a season with 21 in 1985?

30. Name the placekicker who holds the Giants record for field goals in a season with 35.

31. Who was the Giants offensive tackle named as the NFC offensive player of the week following his performance in a 1986 win over the Washington Redskins, 24–14?

32. Which Giants punter holds the team record of 931 punts?

33. Who was voted MVP of Super Bowl XXI?

34. Which position did Bill Parcells play in college at Wichita State University? a. Defensive end b. Linebacker c. Center d. Fullback

35. Who was the defensive end who sacked John Elway in the end zone for a safety in Super Bowl XXI? a. Eric Dorsey b. Leonard Marshall c. George Martin d. John Washington

36. What was the Giants' final won-lost record during the strike-shortened season of 1982? a. 5–4 b. 3–6 c. 4–4–1 d. 4–5

37. Which team did fullback Maurice Carthon play for in the USFL? a. The Boston Breakers b. The Philadelphia Stars c. The New Jersey Generals d. The Houston Gamblers

38. Who was nicknamed Toast by his teammates because he was often burned on pass plays yet still led the team in interceptions in 1985 with six?

39. O. J. Anderson was picked up by the Giants from which NFC team?

40. True or False: Bill Parcells never played in a regular season game in the NFL.

41. What is Jumbo Elliott's given name? a. John b. Jim c. Jerry d. Joseph

42. Who was the Giants general manager before George Young?

43. Which coach said, "The Giants may have been the best all-around team we played all year" after beating them 21–0 in a conference playoff game? a. Joe Gibbs, Washington Redskins b. Tom Landry, Dallas Cowboys c. Bill Walsh, San Francisco 49ers d. Mike Ditka, Chicago Bears

Bill Parcells, the driving force behind the Giants' rebirth. (Jerry Pinkus)

44. How many Giants were named to the Pro Bowl game following the 1986 season? a. 7 b. 5 c. 8 d. 10

45. Who was the Giant who scaled the stadium wall at the Meadowlands to join the fans' celebration after the Giants' shutout victory over the Washington Redskins in the NFC championship game? a. William Roberts b. Jim Burt c. Pepper Johnson d. Andy Headen

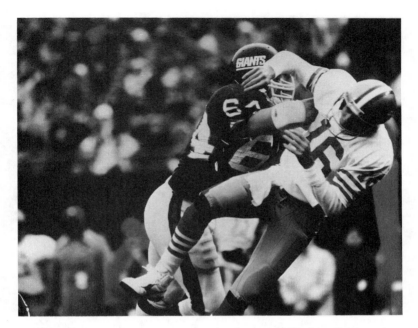

Jim Burt KO's Joe Montana during the Giants' 1987 playoff romp over the San Francisco 49ers on their way to Super Bowl XXI. (Jerry Pinkus)

46. What was the total number of sacks Lawrence Taylor was credited with in 1986, which stands as the Giants single-season record? a. 21 b. 19 c. 20½ d. 21½

47. How many times has Bill Parcells been named NFL Coach of the Year?

48. Who led the Giants in receptions during their championship season in 1986? a. Lionel Manuel b. Mark Bavaro c. Tony Galbreath d. Phil McConkey

49. Which round of the 1985 NFL draft did the Giants select Mark Bavaro? a. Second b. Fifth c. Fourth d. Eighth

50. Who was the losing head coach in Super Bowl XXI?

51. Name the University of Kentucky running back selected by the Giants in the first round of the 1985 draft who quickly went downhill after a productive rookie season.

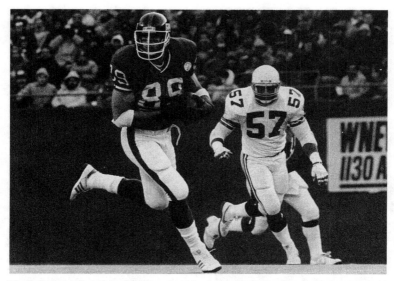

Mark Bavaro lets his All-Pro play do his talking for him. (Jerry Pinkus)

52. What was the site of Super Bowl XXI? a. the Rose Bowl b. Los Angeles Coliseum c. Jack Murphy Stadium in San Diego d. New Orleans Superdome

53. True or False: When Ray Perkins left the Giants he had a career winning record with the team, the first head coach to do so with the Giants since Allie Sherman.

Three of the Greatest

Roosevelt Brown. (New York Giants)

L.T.—Lawrence Taylor, on the prowl. (Jerry Pinkus)

In conjunction with the NFL's 75th anniversary season, a fifteen-member panel of NFL and Pro Football Hall of Fame officials, former players, and members of the media selected an all-time 48-man NFL roster.

Three Giants were named to the squad when the team was announced in August 1994. They were center linebacker Mel Hein, the Giants' greatest iron man from 1931 to 1946; offensive tackle Roosevelt Brown, who played with the Giants from 1953 to 1965 and was a tenacious blocker who would take his place with the defense on goal-line stands; and Lawrence Taylor, number 56, who was with the Giants from 1981 to 1993 and who wrote the book on playing outside linebacker.

Rebirth and Triumph: 1981–90

Answers:

1. Rob Carpenter.

2. False—Parcells was an assistant at Army.

3. 1981.

4. George Rogers, the Heisman Trophy winner from the University of South Carolina. The New Orleans Saints had the first overall pick in the 1981 draft and selected the star running back. The Giants had the second overall pick and selected a defensive end from the University of North Carolina named Lawrence Taylor.

5. b. Joe Danelo.

6. d. Perkins returned to coach at his alma mater, the University of Alabama.

7. c. Byron Hunt.

8. b. The Giants beat the Philadelphia Eagles 27–21.

9. d. 1984.

10. Morris—Syracuse; Bavaro—Notre Dame; Martin—Oregon; Banks—Michigan State; Nelson—Iowa State.

11. a. Pat Summerall.

12. Scott Brunner.

13. #53.

14. George Martin, who scored six touchdowns in his career.

15. c. The Los Angeles Raiders.

16. The Detroit Lions.

17. Maurice Carthon.

18. a. 1985, when Joe Morris gained 1,336 yards.

19. Zeke Mowatt.

20. Mark Haynes.

21. d. Bobby Johnson.

22. Eric Schubert.

23. b. 40 by Phil Simms in a game against the Cincinnati Bengals in 1985.

24. Jim Burt.

25. c. Tony Galbreath.

26. d. The Giants won the game, 17–0.

27. Phil McConkey.

28. b. Butch Woolfolk.

29. Joe Morris.

30. Ali Haji-Sheikh in 1983.

31. Brad Benson was the first offensive lineman so honored.

32. Dave Jennings.

33. Phil Simms.

34. b. Linebacker.

35. c. George Martin.

36. d. The Giants finished 4–5.

37. c. The New Jersey Generals.

38. Elvis Patterson.

39. The St. Louis Cardinals.

40. True. Parcells was drafted by the Detroit Lions in the seventh round of the 1964 draft but was released by them before the end of the exhibition season.

41. a. John.

42. Andy Robustelli.

43. d. Mike Ditka, whose Bears beat the Giants 21–0 in an NFC conference playoff game at Soldier Field in Chicago in 1985.

44. c. 8: Mark Bavaro, Brad Benson, Jim Burt, Harry Carson, Sean Landeta, Leonard Marshall, Joe Morris, and Lawrence Taylor.

45. b. Jim Burt.

46. c. 20½.

47. Once, in 1986, by the *Sporting News*.

48. b. Mark Bavaro led the team in receptions with 66.

49. c. Fourth round—the Giants couldn't believe their good fortune when Bavaro was still available in round four, and they quickly selected him.

50. Dan Reeves.

51. George Adams.

52. a. The Rose Bowl.

53. False—Perkins's record with the Giants was 24–35 during his tenure with the team, spanning the years from 1979 through 1982.

5

On to Super Bowl XXV, and Good-bye, Bill, Hello, Ray: 1991–93

Questions:

1. How many replacement player games, aka scab player games, were played during the 1987 strike season?

2. What was the record of the Giants' replacement players?

3. Karl Nelson retired from football in 1987 due to what illness?

4. Name the basketball coach who was a friend of head coach Bill Parcells's when Parcells was an assistant at Army. a. Bobby Knight b. Joe B. Hall c. Eddie Sutton d. Dick Vitale

5. Name the New York Jets receiver who caught the touchdown pass in the final game of the 1988 season that knocked the Giants out of the playoff race.

6. Which kicker beat the New Orleans Saints with a last minute field goal in a 1988 game? a. Matt Bahr b. Raul Allegre c. Paul McFadden d. George Benyola

7. Which position did Ray Handley play in college? a. Running back b. Defensive back c. Punter d. Wide receiver

8. Have the Giants ever played the Jets in back-to-back seasons?

9. True or False: Despite the strike-shortened season of 1987, Joe Morris still gained more than 1,000 yards rushing.

10. What was the Giants won-lost record in the strike season of 1987? a. 7–8 b. 6–9 c. 7–7–1 d. 10–5

11. Which season did Lawrence Taylor miss the first four games of the season due to a drug suspension?

12. Which L.A. Rams receiver caught a 30-yard touchdown pass in overtime to beat the Giants in a 1989 playoff game?

13. Who was named Most Valuable Player of Super Bowl XXV between the Giants and the Buffalo Bills? a. Phil Simms b. Jeff Hostetler c. Lawrence Taylor d. Ottis Anderson

14. True or False: The Giants won their last four games of the 1990 season, which primed them for their playoff run.

15. Which team did Joe Morris join after leaving the Giants in 1991? a. The Cleveland Browns b. The San Diego Chargers c. The Houston Oilers d. The New York Jets

16. What is Bill Parcells's given name?

17. What is former center Bart Oates's profession off the field?

18. Jeff Hostetler left Penn State to play quarterback at which Big East school? a. Boston College b. University of Miami c. Syracuse University d. University of West Virginia

19. Which Giants linebacker made a game-saving goal-line tackle against Bobby Humphrey of the Denver Broncos in a 1989 game at Denver? a. Lawrence Taylor b. Andy Headen c. Gary Reasons d. Steve DeOssie

20. What position on the coaching staff did Ray Handley hold before he succeeded Bill Parcells as head coach? a. Offensive coordinator b. Defensive backs coach c. Offensive backfield coach d. Special teams coach

21. Who was the Buffalo Bills kicker whose field goal attempt sailed wide to the right in the closing seconds of Super Bowl XXV?

22. Match the player with his alma mater:

John "Jumbo" Elliott	Michigan
Ottis Anderson	Brigham Young
Henry Marshall	Miami (Fla.)
Erik Howard	LSU
Bart Oates	Washington State

23. True or False: Ottis Anderson never had a 1,000-yard-rushing season as a Giant.

24. Phil Simms's 1990 season ended with a sprained foot in the 14th game of the season against which AFC team? a. The New England Patriots b. The Buffalo Bills c. The Cincinnati Bengals d. The Seattle Seahawks

25. Name the former Boston College linebacker and long snapper who the Giants picked up from the Dallas Cowboys before the 1989 season.

26. Which NFL team was Bill Parcells an assistant with before he joined the Giants as a defensive coach in 1981? a. The Philadelphia Eagles b. The St. Louis Cardinals c. The Minnesota Vikings d. The New England Patriots

27. Name the Giants wide receiver who was nicknamed the Touchdown Maker?

28. Name the Giants running back who dashed 89 yards for a touchdown on his first carry as a Giant in a 1990 exhibition game.

29. Nose tackle Jim Burt left the Giants to join which team? a. The Detroit Lions b. The Los Angeles Raiders c. The San Francisco 49ers d. The New Orleans Saints

30. Name the former Giants running back who broke many of Walter Payton's rushing records at Jackson State University.

31. Who was the former Giants defensive coordinator who left in 1991 to take the head coaching job of an AFC team?

32. True or False: Bill Parcells won more than 100 games as head coach of the Giants.

33. Who was the Giants placekicker who nailed five field goals against the San Francisco 49ers in the 1990 NFC championship game, including the game winner as time ran out? a. Raul Allegre b. Matt Stover c. Bjorn Nittmo d. Matt Bahr

34. Who was the former Giants tight end playing with the New England Patriots at the time of a reported incident with a female reporter?

Rodney Hampton—the first Giant to rush for 1,000 in four consecutive seasons. (New York Giants)

35. Name the Giant who scored on a 68-yard punt return in the 1990 season opener against the Philadelphia Eagles.

36. Which former New England Patriots head coach served as Ray Handley's defensive coordinator? a. Raymond Berry b. Rod Rust c. Ron Meyer d. Ron Erhardt

37. Who led the Giants defense with 116 tackles in the 1990 championship season? a. Pepper Johnson b. Lawrence Taylor c. Carl Banks d. Leonard Marshall

38. How many consecutive victories did the Giants attain to start the 1990 season? a. 10   b. 11   c. 8   d. 12

39. Joe Morris's younger brother Jamie was a running back for which NFC East team?

40. What is the position former Giants tight end Mark Bavaro's younger brother David plays in the NFL?

41. True or False: Ray Handley got off on the right foot as Giants head coach by winning the season opener in 1991.

42. Name the former Dallas Cowboy who shored up the Giants defensive backfield for the 1990 season.

43. Which team did the Giants beat 31–3 in a 1990 NFC play-off game? a. The Minnesota Vikings b. The Los Angeles Rams c. The Chicago Bears d. The Washington Redskins

44. In week 15 of the 1990 season the Giants and the Buffalo Bills met at Giants Stadium in what would be a preview of Super Bowl XXV. What was the outcome of that game? a. Bills 19, Giants 17   b. Bills 17, Giants 13   c. Giants 14, Bills 13   d. Bills 16, Giants 14

45. 1988 was the final season for two great Giants defenders who retired. Name them.

46. True or False: Rodney Hampton left the University of Georgia for the NFL draft in 1990 before his college eligibility was finished.

47. Fill in the blanks: In the 1990 championship game, the San Francisco 49ers were leading 13–12 with 2:36 left to play in the game when_____knifed through a block and punched the ball loose from Roger Craig, and_____ recovered the fumble for the Giants to set up the winning field goal.

48. Name the third-string Giants quarterback who came off the bench to throw a dramatic 33-yard pass to Stephen Baker with 21 seconds to play, setting up the winning field goal against the New Orleans Saints in a key game in 1988.

49. How many seasons in the 1980s did the Giants make the playoffs? a. 4 b. 5 c. 3 d. 6

50. Which college team was Bill Parcells head coach of? a. Air Force b. Iowa State c. Army d. Rutgers

51. Which team snapped the Giants' 10-game unbeaten streak in 1990? a. The Dallas Cowboys b. The San Francisco 49ers c. The Washington Redskins d. The Philadelphia Eagles

52. Name the site of Super Bowl XXV, between the Giants and the Buffalo Bills.

53. True or False: In Super Bowl XXV, Buffalo controlled the ball for less than 20 minutes.

54. Which Giants defender's tremendous sack of Joe Montana in the 1990 NFC championship game forced Montana out for the remainder of the game with an injury? a. Carl Banks b. Dave Duerson c. Leonard Marshall d. Lawrence Taylor

55. Who said after winning the 1990 NFC championship game, "They keep telling me I can't do it. Well, I'm going to the Super Bowl"? a. Dave Meggett b. Everson Walls c. Ottis Anderson d. Jeff Hostetler

56. Who coached the Tampa Bay Buccaneers from 1987 to 1990? a. Richard Williamson b. Ray Perkins c. Leeman Bennett d. Buddy Ryan

57. For which network was Bill Parcells a studio analyst after he left the Giants in 1990?

L.T.'s Greatest Game

L.T.'s greatest game: Number 56 causing key fumble in 1988 game against the Saints. (Jerry Pinkus)

In 1988, a battered Giants team traveled down to the Louisiana Superdome to do battle with the New Orleans Saints on Sunday night, November 27. The offense was without Phil Simms, who was nursing bruised ribs, and an untested Jeff Hostetler got the starting nod as quarterback against the then 9–4 Saints.

Lawrence Taylor was also hurting that week thanks to a torn deltoid muscle, but L.T. was determined to play despite the excruciating pain, as the Giants desperately needed the win to stay in the hunt for the NFC East crown. Taylor refused to wear a harness that would decrease the pain, fearing it would limit his mobility.

That Sunday night game under the dome was an offensive coordinator's nightmare. Although the Giants didn't give up any touchdowns in the first half, Saints kicker Morten Anderson booted three field goals. The Saints were also battling for a playoff spot, and their aroused defense constantly stuffed the Giants' ball control offense. The lone Giants score came on a long touchdown pass from Jeff Hostetler to Stephen Baker covering 85 yards. At the half the Giants trailed 9–7.

Taylor fired up the Giants defense in the second half despite the horrible pain that often forced him to the bench during the game. He made seven tackles, had three sacks, and forced two fumbles, both recovered by the Giants. He also had numerous quarterback pressures throughout the game. With 21 seconds to play, Paul McFadden kicked the winning 35-yard field goal to give the Giants a crucial 13–12 win.

After the game Bill Parcells complimented his defensive star by saying, "He was great tonight." When asked if the torn shoulder muscle affected him, L.T. joked, "It slows down my backswing."

Lawrence Taylor was voted NFC player of the week for his efforts in that game. It was typical of what Taylor brought to the Giants game after game, season after season. In 14 years in the NFL covering a career of consistently great play, no one ever accused Lawrence Taylor of a cheap shot or showboating after a sack. Many people believe that the Saints game in 1988, given the severity of his injury, might have been L.T.'s greatest.

ON TO SUPER BOWL XXV AND GOOD-BYE, BILL, HELLO, RAY: 1991–93

Answers:

1. Three.

2. 0–3.

3. Hodgkin's disease.

4. a. Bobby Knight.

5. Al Toon.

6. c. Paul McFadden.

7. a. Ray Handley was a running back at Stanford.

8. Yes, in the final game of the 1987 and 1988 seasons.

9. False—Morris gained 658 yards.

10. b. The Giants finished at 6–9.

11. 1988.

12. Willie "Flipper" Anderson.

13. d. Ottis Anderson.

14. False—the Giants lost three of their last four.

15. a. Joe Morris played for the Cleveland Browns in 1991.

16. Duane Charles Parcells.

17. Bart Oates passed the bar and is an attorney.

18. d. West Virginia.

19. c. Gary Reasons.

20. c. Ray Handley was the Giants offensive backfield coach.

21. Scott Norwood.

22. Elliott—Michigan; Anderson—Miami (Fla.); Marshall—LSU; Howard—Washington State; Oates—Brigham Young.

23. False—Ottis Anderson gained 1,023 yards in 1989.

24. b. The Buffalo Bills.

25. Steve DeOssie.

26. d. Parcells was an assistant coach with the New England Patriots in 1980.

27. Stephen Baker.

28. Rodney Hampton.

29. c. The San Francisco 49ers.

30. Lewis Tillman.

31. Bill Belichick.

32. False—Parcells won 77 games as head coach in his eight-year stint with the Giants.

33. d. Matt Bahr.

34. Zeke Mowatt.

35. Dave Meggett.

36. b. Rod Rust.

37. a. Pepper Johnson.

38. a. 10.

39. The Washington Redskins.

40. Linebacker. He played the 1994 season with the New England Patriots.

41. True—the Giants beat the San Francisco 49ers 16–14 at the Meadowlands.

42. Everson Walls.

43. c. The Chicago Bears.

44. b. The Bills won, 17–13.

45. Harry Carson and George Martin.

46. True.

47. Erik Howard, Lawrence Taylor.

48. Jeff Rutledge.

49. b. Five: 1981, 1984, 1985, 1986, and 1989.

50. a. Parcells was head coach of the Air Force Academy, leading the Falcons to a 3–8 record in 1978.

51. d. The Philadelphia Eagles beat the Giants 31–13 in Philadelphia.

52. Tampa Stadium, Tampa, Florida.

53. True—Buffalo's time of possession was 19 minutes and 27 seconds.

54. c. Leonard Marshall.

55. d. Jeff Hostetler.

56. b. Ray Perkins.

57. NBC.

6

GOOD-BYE, RAY, HELLO, DAN: 1993–94

Questions:

1. What was Ray Handley's record in his first season as head coach?

2. Who did Mike Sherrard play with before he came to the Giants in 1993? a. The Dallas Cowboys b. The San Francisco 49ers c. The Denver Broncos d. The Phoenix Cardinals

3. True or False: Rodney Hampton was the first Giants back to have four consecutive 1,000-yard-rushing seasons?

4. Which running back made his NFL debut in the 1992 season opener against the Giants with a 100-yard effort? a. Randy Baldwin, Minnesota b. Eric Bieniemy, San Diego c. Ricky Watters, San Francisco d. Edgar Bennett, Green Bay

5. Who is the Giants' all-time leading scorer? a. Pete Gogolak b. Pat Summerall c. Frank Gifford d. Ken Strong

6. Who was Ray Handley's first choice as quarterback to begin his first season as head coach in 1991?

7. For which team did Dan Reeves play professional football?

8. The lone Giants 1993 playoff win was against which team? a. The Washington Redskins b. The Detroit Lions c. The Green Bay Packers d. The Minnesota Vikings

9. Who led the Giants in sacks in 1991? a. Pepper Johnson b. Lawrence Taylor c. Leonard Marshall d. Corey Miller

10. Which team did Carl Banks sign with in 1993 after leaving the Giants? a. The Washington Redskins b. The Detroit Lions c. The Cleveland Browns d. The Cincinnati Bengals

11. After falling behind 34–0 in this 1992 game, the Giants scored four touchdowns on four consecutive possessions

but came up short 34–28. Who was the team they lost to?
a. The Denver Broncos b. The Dallas Cowboys c. The Phoenix Cardinals d. The Buffalo Bills

12. Which school is Dan Reeves's alma mater? a. University
of Alabama b. University of Colorado c. University of South
Carolina d. University of Pittsburgh

13. His father was a Giants defensive back in the 1950s and
early 1960s, and he is currently Dan Reeves's defensive coordinator. Who is he?

14. Who was the Giants' first-round pick in the 1991 NFL
draft?

15. Which linebacker led the New York Giants in tackles in
1993? a. Corey Miller b. Carlton Bailey c. Michael Brooks
d. Lawrence Taylor

16. True or False: Phil Simms was named to the NFC Pro
Bowl after the 1993 season.

17. In 1992, Rodney Hampton ran for a then-career-high 167
yards in a game against which team? a. The Seattle Seahawks
b. The Indianapolis Colts c. The Atlanta Falcons d. The
Phoenix Cardinals

18. Name the two other candidates who were considered for
the Giants head-coaching job before Dan Reeves was chosen.

19. How many times have the Giants won the NFL championship?

20. What was Ray Handley's record as Giants head coach?

21. Which two members of the Giants' victorious Super Bowl
XXV team played with the Jets in 1993?

22. Name the Giants back whose longest run from scrimmage—51 yards—occurred in the 1993 playoff game against
the Minnesota Vikings.

23. True or False: Dan Reeves has never been on a winning
Super Bowl team as either a player or a coach.

24. Who caught a one-yard touchdown pass from Phil Simms with 1:07 to play in the 1993 season opener, enabling the Giants to beat the Bears in Chicago? a. Jarrod Bunch b. Lewis Tillman c. Ed McCaffrey d. Howard Cross

25. Which Giant threw two passes in 1993, both for touchdowns?

26. Match the player with his alma mater:

Howard Cross	South Carolina
Corey Miller	Duke
Mike Sherrard	Pittsburgh
Keith Hamilton	Alabama
Dave Brown	UCLA

27. Name the sure-handed Giants receiver who led the team in receptions in 1992 with 49 and was later picked up by the San Francisco 49ers after the Giants released him in 1994.

28. The Giants played an exhibition in the summer of 1994 against the San Diego Chargers in which European city? a. Berlin b. Barcelona c. London d. Paris

29. Which member of the Giants' winning Super Bowl team of 1986 ran for Congress?

30. Who filled in most ably for an injured Rodney Hampton by running for 169 yards and two touchdowns in a 21–10 Giants win over the Philadelphia Eagles in a 1993 contest?

31. Who led the Giants in sacks in 1993 with 11½? a. Corey Miller b. Stacey Dillard c. Michael Brooks d. Keith Hamilton

32. Name the two defensive backs the Giants selected in the 1994 NFL draft.

33. Which former Giants player said league commissioner Paul Tagliabue should be tested for drugs after the NFL commissioner commented about the salary cap's effect on that player's career?

34. Where is the Giants training camp located?

35. Name the All-Pro inside linebacker the Giants signed from the Denver Broncos before the 1993 season.

36. This player's 1992 season ended earlier than he would have liked, thus prompting a return for the 1993 season despite original plans to retire. Who is he?

37. Which team scored 34 consecutive points against the Giants in a 1992 defeat of New York, 47–34? a. The Dallas Cowboys b. The Philadelphia Eagles c. The San Francisco 49ers d. The Miami Dolphins

38. Which team have the Giants faced the most times since their inception? a. The Philadelphia Eagles b. The Washington Redskins c. The Chicago Bears d. The Dallas Cowboys

39. This undersized Ivy Leaguer came off the campus at Princeton to win a spot with the Giants in 1994. Who is he?

40. Which team did the Giants hand their worst loss to in 45 years by way of a 41–7 blowout in a 1993 game at this team's home field? a. The Detroit Lions b. The Green Bay Packers c. The Pittsburgh Steelers d. The Washington Redskins

41. Who kicked the game-winning 54-yard field goal with 32 seconds left against the Phoenix Cardinals, making it, at that time, only his third NFL field goal?

42. Which team did the Giants beat in 1993, snapping that ball club's 11-game winning streak against NFC East division teams? a. The Miami Dolphins b. The San Francisco 49ers c. The Los Angeles Raiders d. The Kansas City Chiefs

43. Rodney Hampton rushed for a career-high 173 yards in a 1993 game against which team? a. The Los Angeles Rams b. The Cleveland Browns c. The Indianapolis Colts d. The San Diego Chargers

44. Name the running back who carried the ball 32 times for 168 yards in his team's 16–13 overtime win over the Giants in the final game of the 1993 regular season.

45. Who was the last Giant to lead the NFC in passing?

Phil Simms, a pro's pro. (New York Giants)

46. Who is the Giants' all-time leading rusher?

47. Who is the Giants' all-time leader in touchdowns?

48. True or False: Dan Reeves was voted NFL Coach of the Year in 1993 by the Pro Football Writers of America, the *Associated Press,* the *Sporting News, Pro Football News,* and the Maxwell Club.

49. Which Giant was voted NFC special teams player of the month for November 1993? a. Dave Meggett b. Jesse Armstead c. Corey Widmer d. Aaron Pierce

50. How many times since 1925 have the Giants reached postseason play?

51. How many touchdown passes did Phil Simms retire with?

52. How many times have the Giants led the NFL in fewest points allowed? a. 10 times b. 9 times c. 12 times d. 6 times

53. In the 1994 season opener against the Philadelphia Eagles, Dave Meggett returned a punt for a touchdown, helping the Giants to a 28–23 win. How many times in an NFL game has Dave Meggett returned punts for touchdowns? a. Nine b. Four c. Six d. Five

54. Who caught Dave Brown's first NFL touchdown pass in the season opener against the Philadelphia Eagles? a. Dave Meggett b. Chris Calloway c. Howard Cross d. Kenyon Rasheed

55. Which Pittsburgh Steeler running back gained over 100 yards against the Giants in a 1994 game?

56. The Giants snapped a seven-game losing streak in 1994 against which AFC team? a. The Pittsburgh Steelers b. The Houston Oilers c. The Cleveland Browns d. The Cincinnati Bengals

57. Who was the rookie from Kansas State University who sparkled in the Giants defensive secondary in 1994?

58. How many Giants played in the 1995 Pro Bowl?

59. Lawrence Taylor's jersey, number 56, was retired at halftime in a *Monday Night Football* game against which NFC team? a. The Minnesota Vikings b. The Detroit Lions c. The Dallas Cowboys d. The Philadelphia Eagles

60. How many playoff teams did the Giants beat during the 1994 season?

61. Dave Meggett threw an option pass for a touchdown against which NFC rival in 1994?

62. For which network does former great Phil Simms now work as an analyst?

63. For which network did former great Lawrence Taylor work as an analyst?

64. What was head coach Dan Reeves' preseason prediction for the Giants in 1994? a. Ten wins and six losses b. Nine wins and seven losses c. Twelve wins and four losses d. Three wins and thirteen losses

65. Who was the Giants wide receiver who was called for a controversial taunting penalty in a key loss to the New Orleans Saints in 1994?

GOOD-BYE, RAY, HELLO, DAN: 1993–94

Answers:

1. 8–8.

2. b. The San Francisco 49ers.

3. True.

4. c. Ricky Watters of San Francisco.

5. a. Pete Gogolak.

6. Jeff Hostetler.

7. The Dallas Cowboys, from 1965–72.

8. d. The Giants beat the Minnesota Vikings 17–10 at the Meadowlands.

9. c. Leonard Marshall, with 11 sacks.

10. a. The Washington Redskins.

11. b. The Dallas Cowboys.

12. c. The University of South Carolina.

13. Mike Nolan (his father was Giants defensive back Dick Nolan).

14. Jarrod Bunch, fullback, University of Michigan.

15. Carlton Bailey, with 136 tackles.

16. True, but due to an injury he did not play.

17. d. The Phoenix Cardinals at Giants Stadium.

18. Tom Coughlin and Dave Wannstedt.

19. Six: 1927, 1934, 1938, 1956, 1986, and 1990.

20. 14–18.

21. Leonard Marshall and Steve DeOssie.

22. Rodney Hampton.

23. False—Dan Reeves was a member of two Super Bowl winning teams: in Super Bowl VI he was a player with the Dallas Cowboys, and in Super Bowl XII he was an assistant coach for the Cowboys.

24. a. Jarrod Bunch.

25. Dave Meggett.

26. Cross—Alabama; Miller—South Carolina; Sherrard—UCLA; Hamilton—Pittsburgh; Brown—Duke.

27. Ed McCaffrey.

28. a. Berlin.

29. Phil McConkey.

30. Lewis Tillman.

31. d. Keith Hamilton.

32. Thomas Randolph, a cornerback from Kansas State University, and Jason Sehorn, a safety from USC.

33. Phil Simms.

34. Fairleigh Dickinson University–Madison campus, Madison, New Jersey.

35. Michael Brooks.

36. Lawrence Taylor.

37. b. The Philadelphia Eagles.

38. a. The Philadelphia Eagles. The Giants and the Eagles have played one another 122 times, with the Giants owning a slight edge in the series.

39. Keith Elias.

40. d. The Washington Redskins.

41. Brad Daluiso.

42. a. The Miami Dolphins.

43. c. The Indianapolis Colts.

44. Emmitt Smith.

45. Phil Simms, in 1990.

46. Joe Morris, with 5,296 yards.

47. Frank Gifford, with 78 touchdowns.

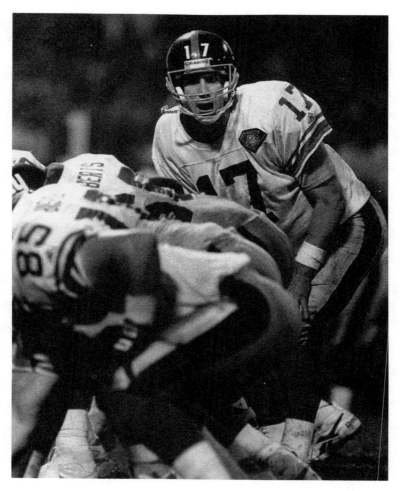

The Giants' new trigger-man, quarterback Dave Brown. (Jerry Pinkus)

48. True.

49. b. Jesse Armstead.

50. 23 times, an NFL record.

51. 199.

52. a. 10 times, an NFL record.

53. d. Five.

54. b. Chris Calloway.

55. Byron "Bam" Morris.

56. b. The Houston Oilers.

57. Thomas Randolph.

58. No New York Giant was selected for the 1995 Pro Bowl.

59. a. The Minnesota Vikings.

60. Two: The Dallas Cowboys and the Cleveland Browns.

61. The Washington Redskins.

62. NBC.

63. TNT.

64. b. Nine wins and seven losses—Reeves was right on the mark.

65. Chris Calloway.

Giants Record Holders Over the Years

Individual Records—Career

Rushing Yards	Joe Morris, 1982–88	5,296
Passing Yards	Phil Simms, 1979–93	33,462
Passing Touchdowns	Phil Simms, 1979–93	199
Receptions	Joe Morrison, 1959–72	395
Receiving Yards	Frank Gifford, 1952–64	5,434
Interceptions	Emlen Tunnell, 1948–58	74
Punting Average	Don Chandler, 1956–64	43.8
Punt Return Average	Dave Meggett, 1989–94	10.8
Kickoff Return Average	Rocky Thompson, 1971–72	27.2
Field Goals	Pete Gogolak, 1966–74	126
Touchdowns	Frank Gifford, 1952–64	78
Points	Pete Gogolak, 1966–74	646
Sacks	Lawrence Taylor, 1981–93	132½

Individual Records—Single Season

Rushing Yards	Joe Morris, 1986	1,516
Passing Yards	Phil Simms, 1984	4,004
Passing Touchdowns	Y. A. Tittle, 1963	36
Receptions	Earnest Gray, 1983	78
Receiving Yards	Homer Jones, 1967	1,209
Interceptions	Otto Schnellbacher, 1951	11
	Jim Patton, 1958	11
Punting Average	Don Chandler, 1959	46.6
Punt Return Average	Merle Hapes, 1942	15.5
Kickoff Return Average	John Salscheider, 1949	31.6
Field Goals	Ali Haji-Sheikh, 1983	35
Points	Ali Haji-Sheikh, 1983	127
Touchdowns	Joe Morris, 1985	22
Sacks	Lawrence Taylor, 1986	20½

Individual Records—Single Game

Rushing Yards	Gene "Choo-Choo" Roberts, 11/12/50	218
Passing Yards	Phil Simms, 10/13/85	513
Passing Touchdowns	Y. A. Tittle, 10/28/62	7
Receptions	Mark Bavaro, 10/13/85	12
Receiving Yards	Del Shofner, 10/28/62	269
Interceptions	Many players	3
	Last time by Terry Kinnard, 9/27/87	
Touchdowns	Ron Johnson, 10/2/72	4
	Earnest Gray, 9/7/80	4
Field Goals	Joe Danelo, 10/18/81	6
Points	Ron Johnson, 10/2/72	24
	Earnest Gray, 9/7/80	24

Sam Huff. (Dan Rubin)